Godly Tendencies

VOLUME 4

ALAN HINES

 www.trafford.com

North America & international
toll-free: 844-688-6899 (USA & Canada)
fax: 812 355 4082

1. Founded Love (Volume 1, 2, and 3)
2. True Love (Volume 1, 2, and 3)
3. Love (Endless Volumes)
4. Tormented Tears (Volume 1, 2, and 3)
5. A Inner Soul That Cried (Volume 1, 2, and 3)
6. Visionary (Endless Volumes)
7. A Seed That Grew (Volume 1, 2, and, 3)
8. The Words I Spoke (Volume 2, and 3)
9. Scriptures (Volume 1, 2, and 3)
10. Revelations (volume 1, 2, and 3)
11. Destiny (Volume 1, 2, and 3)
12. Trials and Tribulations (Volume 1, 2, and 3)
13. IMMORTALITY (Volume 1,2, and 3)
14. My Low Spoken Words (Volume 1, 2, and 3)
15. Beauty Within (Volume 1, 2, and 3)
16. Red Ink of Blood (Volume 1, 2, and 3)
17. Destiny of Light (Jean Hines) (Volume 1, 2, and 3)
18. Deep Within (Volume 1, 2, and 3)
19. Literature (Volume 1, 2, and 3)
20. Silent Mind (Volume 1, 2, and 3)
21. Amor (Volume 1, 2, and 3)
22. Joyce (Volume 1, 2, and 3)
23. Lovely Joyce (Volume 1, 2, and 3)
24. Pink Lady (Volume 1, 2, and 3)
25. Mockingbird Lady (Volume 1, 2, and 3)
26. Enchanting Arrays (Volume 1, 2, and 3)
27. Harmony (Volume 1, 2, and 3)
28. Realism (Volume 1, 2, and 3)
29. Manifested Deep Thoughts (Volume 1, 2, and 3)
30. Poectic Lines of Scrimage (Volume 1, 2, and 3)
31. Garden of Love (Volume 1, 2, and 3)
32. Reflection In The Mirror. (Volume 1, 2, and 3)

UPCOMING NON-FICTION BOOKS BY ALAN HINES,

1. Time Versus Life
2. Timeless Jewels
3. The Essence of Time
4. Memoirs of My Life
5. In my Eyes To See
6. A Prisoner's Black History

UPCOMING URBAN NOVELS BY ALAN HINES,

1. Black Kings
2. Playerlistic
3. The Police
4. Scandalous Scandal
5. The West Side Rapist
6. Shattered Dreams
7. She Wrote Murder
8. Black Fonz
9. A Slow Form of Suicide
10. No Motherfucking Love
11. War Stories
12. Race against time
13. Ghetto Heros
14. Boss Pimps
15. Adolescents
16. In The Hearts of Men
17. Story Teller
18. Kidnapping
19. Mob Ties

ACKNOWLEDGEMENTS

Thanking the Heavenly Father for all his many blessings which includes me being able to write and publish another book.

1. THE GRAVITY

The gravity, of gravitation.
We must crawl before we walk,
standing ovation.
Walking the tightrope, freely to float.
Continue to grow.
Love from our father, his children,
love's Goat.

2. A WILL, A WAY

Where there is a will, there's a way.
Pray for better days.
Follow the Lord never go astray.
In your heart and mind allow God to live to stay.
Love more on any ordinary day.
Love, live, pray.
Know that there is a will,
there's a way, if you believe in God,
and pray.

3. GIVE ME

Give me sight.
Give me delight.
Give me a way of will,
and might.

4. JESUS NAME

In Jesus name I pray.
I pray for better days.

In Jesus name I pray.
Pray that after the storms and rain
the sun shall shine my way.

In Jesus name I pray.
I pray that I wont go astray.

In Jesus name I pray.

5. COOLING AWAY

Cooling away.
Loving away.
Pleasing away.
Caring away.

6. THE ONLY

The only of life of time.
The only God that gives light
to stages of blind.
The only God to rule mankind the creator,
of love, life, loyalty combine.

7. LOVE HOWEVER

A pleasure I know that Heaven only get's better.
An angelic angel wings, feather.
Love However.

8. LOVELY LOVE COMBINE

Lovely love combine.
Sweet lady of daily Valentine make love to my mind.
Release me from trouble I can't find.
Be my peace, my peace of mind.

9. READ IT

Read the scriptures of Deuteronomy, Proverbs, Psalms
to get through lifetime, breeze through your mind.
Be that of written scriptures holy, and divine.
Love mankind.

Read, read Genesis, Romans, and Revelation,
honor God know he's coming back so just have patients.

10. I TESTIFY

I testify that God gave me the gift
of life as this morning I opened my eyes.

I testify that those that backslide and never come back to
to God, and Christ shall feel the wrath and never make it
to Heavenly Paradise.

I testify to goodness of God's light,
as my prayers take flight.

11. LOVE TO LIVE

Love to live.
Love to reach paradise upon demise.

Love spread.
Love as nourishment, nutrition,
calcium well fed.

Love to lead,
love led.

12. RED

Red.

Red, she was the best love
I ever had.
Her lipstick and fingernails,
and toe nails polish was red.
Happy never sad.
She'd care for others as they was going
through troublesome time she'd
wipe away the tears they shed.

Red, the best love I ever had,
she'd study law to prosecute
the crooked cops, and Feds.

Red, her liberty colors were blue,
white and red instead.

My love of color of time,
color of peace,
color of unity, red.

13. BUT I LOVE

But I love, loving you.
Shall honor you, put no one above you.

14. KING GOD

King God.
Thanks for making love large.
Please give freedom for the wrongfully convicted,
that's behind bars.
Continue to love your seeded, children thus far.

King God.

15. THE

The love.
The life.
The eternity.

16. SAY YOUR GRACE

Say your grace.
"God is good in each and every way."

Say a prayer each day.
"In Jesus name we pray."

Glorify thou Heavenly Father's name
without shame.

17. LOVE TO REMAIN

Love to remain.
The best as it came.
Love to substain.

18. LORD USE ME

Lord use me for what I'm worth.
To sing, make music poetry of
you works to surround be spreaded
across the Earth.

Use me for what I'm worth
as a plated seed to grow
beyond the mud, dirt.

Lord let your will be done as it
is in Heaven on Earth.

Use me for what I'm worth.

19. CHRIST LIFE

Christ.
After life.
Paradise.
Christ life.

20. THE GOSPEL OF GOD

The gospel of God;
made life pleasurable
instead of being hard.

The love of God
is great beyond the stars.

Love God, but at the same time,
love who you be who you are.

21. A VERSE

A verse.
Love being dispersed.

A verse of knowledge.
We are a reflection of God,
being marvelous.

A verse a tool,
love it to use.

22. THE LOVE, THE LIFE

The love, my life.
My Earthly paradise.
She keep's me closer to God,
closer to Christ.
A great sense of delight.
Soaring above all heights.

My love, the love of my life.
Earthly Paradise.

23. BE BLESSED

Be blessed.
Leave it in God's hands less stress.

Be great.
Pray to reach the pearly gates.

24. LOVE YOU

Love you.
Put no one above you.

Cherish.
Love you without being jealous.

25. TO REST

To rest.
To live.
To give.
It is what it is.

26. GOD, LARGE

God.
Large.
Above Jupiter and Mars.
The Alpha and Omega you are.

27. LOVE OF LIFE

The love of life.
Gave me life.
Forgiving me for possessing imperfections within sin,
through his son Christ.

The love of life.

28. WORSHIP

Worship.
Adore you.
Love you.

29. LOVE STAY

Love stay.
Love my way.
Love's enchanting array.

30. LOVE'S DELIGHT

Ignite.
Enlight.
Spark of love's delight.

31. GLORIFY THOU NAME

Who am I to complain.
Instead I just glorify thou name.

32. IN MIND, IN TIME

In mind.
In time.
Love thou father, the
inventor of mankind.

33. FLY HIGH

Fly high.
Live life through the
truth not a lie.
Worship God faithfully until demise.

34. BRING

Bring.
Bring forth messages of the truth.
Love righteous growth as a fruit.
Love unto.
Bring forth all the goodness that's due.

35. BELIEVE IN GOD

Believe in God.
Live out dreams.
Be a reflection of the king of kings.

36. AFTER PRAYER

After prayer hold your head up,
uprise, born again baptize honor our
father whom are in Heaven above the skies.

37. DO IT BIG

Do it big, live, learn, and
dream.
Let freedom ring like the late
great husband of Coretta Scott King.

38. THERE

There she is my lady of years.

There she go a love I never want to let go.

There she shine the essence of time.

39. WITH HER

To be with her.
For her I adore.
Love galore.
Lovely within beauty and more.
Love to love her.

40. LOVER'S DELIGHT

Sunlight.
Sunny delight.
Love's appetite.
Lovely as a delight.
A lover's delight.

41. AMAZING GRACE

Amazing grace.
Amazing touch.
Amazing love by the bunch.

42. ROLE MODEL

Free you mind,
prayer to be free from sorrow.
Ahead of time thank God for a better
day tomorrow.
Love our father in the likeness of himself,
role model.

43. SEE WHO YOU ARE

See who you are, you're my superstar.
Super is who you are.
Shine bright like the north star.
Love who you are.
Love honest, and true, my superstar you are.

44. PROUD TO BE

Divine.
Fine.
Aged like wine.
Proud to be mines.

45. IF I

If I was your's and you were mines.
We would do things that only came to
heart and mind.

If I was your's and you were mines
we'd be together until the end of time.

46. LISTEN TO

Listen to the songs in which the people sing.
The chorus representing God, My king.
Love as it seems.
A pleasant bell that rings.

Listen to the people that sing.
All hail to the new born king.

47. IN A TIME

In a love.
In love.
Is love.
God is Love.

48. THE LOVE

Happy feelings.
Wonderful feelings.
The love that stand taller than buildings.

49. IN MIND INCLINED

In mind.
Spiritually inclined.
The inventor and life, within time.

50. WE MUST

We must continue to live, breathe.
Shackles of chains setting free.
For I am you, you are me.

51. BE MARVELOUS

Prosper.
Be marvelous.
Share, share love regardless.

52. COME WITH ME

Come with me.
Be with me.
Falling in love for love to see.

53. PART OF

Part of me, my identity.
Set me free.
Be the trees of growthly
time we need to breathe.

Part of me, my identity.

54. COMPLETION

Your love stand tall.
Completion, entirely.
For I am you, you are me.

55. LOVE MATTERS

Love matters.
Your existence matters.
Your life matters.
Your love matters.

56. PROMISES

Promises.
I promise that today I'll love you more tomorrow.

Promises.
I promise to get better in time as we shine.

Promises.
I promise my love will last ever more in the days
of tomorrow.

57. PRAY FOR

Pray for time within love.

Pray that angels will be your guardian's from up above.

Pray that together we shall ever more love.

58. FEELINGS

Feelings to show.
Feelings to grow.
Feelings to constantly flow.

59. PIANOS AND FLUTES

Pianos and flutes.
Harmonizing melodies of love unto.
Winds that blew.
Cheers, here's to loving you.
Female guru.

60. LOVE LACED

Love laced.
Love just in case.
Love by God's grace.
Love that can't be replaced.

61. CAN'T GET

Can't get you out of my mind.
Love all the time.
Love as rhythm, a rhyme.
Love all the time.
Love the way you shine.

62. YOU

Kissing you.
Missing you.
Loving you.

63. GAIN

Gain.
Substain.
My everything.
Supreme.
Reality of a sweet dream.
My queen.

64. MODELED

Your heart and mind follow.
Happiness modeled.
My love, lovely and marvelous.

65. LOVE EACH OTHER

Love.
Long as we got each other.
Love one another.
Love further.

Love.

66. GLAMOUR

The glamour, the lights.
Delight.
Gave me sight.
The mother of Earth, nature of life.

67. REALIZE

Realize.
Love's enterprise.
Love that lies.
Love to forever rely.

68. HOME

Home.
Love to live all along.
Love carry on.
A house of love built
of spiritual stone.

Home.
Love long.

69. TRUST THE

Trust the time.
Trust the frame.
Trust the love safety
protection to remain.
Trust God one in the same.

70. LISTEN TO

Listen to the people sing.
Shine a diamond ring.
Be supreme.
Be my queen.
To me you mean the world in it's entirety,
everything.

71. I THANK GOD THAT

I thank God that I got a peace of
mind one more time.
Love at all times.

I thank God that I got a peace of mind,
for making me a champion of mountains to climb.

I thank God that I got a peace of mind,
from him love designed, guidance in time.

I thank God I got a peace of mind.

72. LOVE, LIVE, LONG

Love, live, long.
Blessed still be here.
In God we trust,
and only him we shall fear.

73. PEACE BE

Peace be multiplied.
Awakening of eyes.
Eternal life to reside.
Love that lies.

74. LOVELY SHOWING

Lovely and glowing.
Love showing.
Lovely, love flowing.

75. GOD IS IN CONTROL

God is in control.
God bless your soul.
God's love shall continue to grow.

God is in control.

76. THE LOVE, LIFE

The love.
The life.
The loyalty.
Lovely as can be.
Lovely and free.
Lovely, wonderful to me.

77. A FATHER

The beginning, the end.
Love with no end.
Forgiveness for sins.
A father, a best friend.

78. TO LIVE

To live is to be.
To love, to love free.
To grow as a planted seed.

79. THE LORD

The Lord of life.
The Lord of living.
The Lord of faith.
The Lord of giving.
The Lord of times.
The Lord of privilege.

80. LOVE CLEAR

To love.
To fear.
Love clear.

81. A POSITIVE

A positive, motivating force in my life.
Eternal peace, eternal love,
and paradise.

82. CRYSTAL BALL

Crystal ball.
Statue of liberty of love to stand tall.
Love in it's entirety all.
Crystal ball of love, love all.

83. FEELINGS RIGHT

Feelings right.
Love making in the days,
and night.
Delight.
Feed my love's appetite.
Stand tall love's will and might.

84. THE MYSTERY

The magic.
The mystery.
The love's in the air.
To touch, to feel, to see.

85. ADORE YOU

I adore you.
I love you.
I feel you.
For as one I am you.

86. LOVE APPRAISE

Love always.
Love appraise.
Love you more each day.
Love appraise.

87. AN ANGEL'S

I'm taking by an angel's twin.
Love within.
My super friend.
Love letters of love
with no end.
An angel's twin.

88. LOVE SUPREME

Love supreme.
Love queen.
Lovely human being.
Love that gleams.

89. CREST

Crest.
Bless.
Love nest.
Loving the tenderness of your caress.

90. SOUL OF LOVE

Soul of love, peace, rest.
Love until my last breath.
Souls caring, as peace rest.
Love, to live to love
the soul within the Earthly flesh.

91. LOVE TO LIVE LIFE

Love of life.
New life.
Love to live life.

92. LOVE LIVES ON

Love lives on.
Love all full grown.
Love as a pleasure tone.

93. FLOWN

Flown like a love of a kite.
Blown like a cool breeze of time versus life.
Love as a great sense of delight.

94. LOVE ABOVE

Love above average.
Lavish.
Love palace.
Love satisfying.

95. LOVE GRAND

Grand.
Grand stand.
Love stand.
Love immortal
throught the son of man.

96. ENERGY

Energy.
Plenty.
Infinite.
Loving she.

97. ABOVE CLOUDS

Above clouds.
Love out loud.
Love I'm proud.

98. FELL IN LOVE

Fall in love.
Fell in love.
Love being in love.

99. THE WORLD TO ME

Mean the world to me.
Love she be.
Love to ever more be.
Love freed.

She mean's the world to me.

100. LOVE'S PARADISE

Into my life.
Paradise.

Love that gives us life.
Paradise.

Love to be free
as spirits take flight.
Paradise.

Printed in the United States
by Baker & Taylor Publisher Services